VIJAYA KUMAR

New Dawn

NEW DAWN
a division of Sterling Publishers (P) Ltd.
A-59, Okhla Industrial Area, Phase-II, New Delhi-110020
Tel: 26387070, 26386209
Fax: 91-11-26383788
E-mail: ghai@nde.vsnl.net.in
www.sterlingpublishers.com

108 Names of Hanuman
© 2003, Sterling Publishers Private Limited
ISBN 81 207 2024 5

Reprint 2007

All rights are reserved. No part of this publication may be reproduced, stored in a retrieval system or transmitted, in any form or by any means, mechanical, photocopying, recording or otherwise, without prior written permission of the original publisher.

Published by Sterling Publishers Pvt. Ltd., New Delhi-110020.
Lasertypeset by Vikas Compographics, New Delhi-110020.
Printed at Sterling Publisher Pvt. Ltd., New Delhi-110 020

Preface

Lord Hanuman is a popular and favourite deity of the masses. Known for his loyalty and devoted services to Lord Rama, he can fly and change form at will. He is worshipped as 'Sankat Mochan', one who dispels distress, and brings happiness.

Following the tradition of celebrating the holy names of God, we have chosen 108 names, signifying of the 108 beads in a rosary.

Chanting God's names evokes in us a religious fervour, and helps us to focus on the Almighty.

Vijaya Kumar

Anjaneya

ॐ श्री आंजनेयाय नमः

Son Of Anjani

The great Son of Anjani and Kesari, the illustrious Son of Wind-God (and the noble Son of Lord Shiva) Lord Hanuman's glory and brilliance are illimitable, and He is truly worthy of worship.

Mahavira

ॐ श्री महावीराय नमः
Most Valiant

The scourge of the enemy, Lord Hanuman not only successfully defends His army against vicious demons like Ravana, but every time there is a crisis, it is He who diffuses it and helps Lord Rama.

Hanumat

ॐ श्री हनुमते नमः
Puffy Cheeks

The strong and sturdy Son of Wind-God, Lord Hanuman is a lovable deity. His puffy cheeks and pink eyes endear Him to the masses.

Marutatmaja

ॐ श्री मारूतात्मजाय नमः

Most Beloved Like Gems

Being a mine of all virtues, Lord Hanuman is the most beloved deity of many, treasured and worshipped like the gems that attract all. His effectiveness and capabilities are renowned the world over.

Tatvagnyanaprada

ॐ श्री तत्वज्ञानप्रदाय नमः

Granter Of Wisdom

Endowed with an ocean of intelligence, Lord Hanuman serves His Lord Rama. He blesses his devotees with wisdom – the knowledge of the divine.

Sitadevi Mudrapradayaka

ॐ श्री सीतादेवी मुद्राप्रदायकाय नमः

Deliverer Of The Ring To Sita

Lord Hanuman, noted for His devoted services to Lord Rama, delivered the ring given by Lord Rama, as a token of identification, to Sita in Lanka.

Ashokavanikachhetrey

ॐ श्री अशोकवनिकच्छेत्रै नमः

Destroyer Of Ashoka Grove

When Lord Hanuman found Sita in the Ashoka grove, He created a lot of havoc, uprooting trees, eating all the fruits, and killing the guards there, thus inviting the wrath of Ravana.

Sarvamayavibhanjana

ॐ श्री सर्वमायाविभंजनाय नमः

Destroyer Of All Illusions

The large-hearted, exalted God, Lord Hanuman, is the destroyer of all illusions, and does this while He changes His form several times.

Sarvabandhavimoktri

ॐ श्री सर्वबंधविमोक्त्रे नमः

Liberates From All 'Bondings'

Born to Mother Anjani and sired by Vayu, Wind-God, Lord Hanuman is a confirmed bachelor who skilfully detaches all relationships.

Rakshovidhwansakaraka

ॐ श्री रक्षोविध्वंसकारकाय नमः

Slayer Of Demons

Lord Hanuman slays all the arrogant demons easily, and destroys all wicked tendencies. He is supremely powerful and capable of vanquishing the greatest of enemies.

Paravidhyaparihara

ॐ श्री परविद्यापरिहाराय नमः

Destroyer Of Enemies' Wisdom

Lord Hanuman, the most virtuous, strong and valiant among the monkey clan, is the destroyer of His enemies' wisdom, which He does by assuming any form to His advantage.

Parashaurya Vinashana

ॐ श्री परशौर्य विनाशनाय नमः

Destroyer Of Enemy's Valour

Undaunted by the presence of many demons in the court of Ravana, Lord Hanuman very boldly defies Ravana, thus resulting in His tail being set on fire. Consequently he set Lanka on fire, thus destroying His enemies' valour.

Paramantra Nirakartri

ॐ श्री परमन्त्र निराकर्त्रै नमः

Acceptor Of Rama's Mantra Only

Lord Hanuman loves to hear chanting of the name of Lord Rama who is the Omniscient God. He coalesces with His God, and becomes one with Him.

Parayantra Prabhedaka

ॐ श्री परयन्त्र प्रभेदकाय नमः

Destroyer Of Enemies' Missions

By the grace of Lord Rama, the valiant monkey Lord Hanuman destroys all His enemies' missions with His thunderbolt-like mace, supernatural strength and cleverness.

Sarvagraha Nivashin

ॐ श्री सर्वग्रह निवाशिने नमः

Killer Of Evil Effects Of Planets

Lord Hanuman is the antidote for the evil influence of the planets. As He is beyond any evil effect of the planets, He protects His devotees against them too.

Bheemasenasahayakrut

ॐ श्री भीमसेनासहायकृते नमः

Helper Of Bheema

When Lord Hanuman cures Bheema of his arrogance, the latter entreats Him to help him in the war against the Kauravas in the battle of Kurukshetra.

Sarvaduhkhahara

ॐ श्री सर्वदुःखसहाय नमः

Reliever Of All Agonies

The distress-dispelling Lord Hanuman grants every desire of His devotees, and is the fulfilment of material wants. He is the granter of salvation to the soul, and provides shelter for His devotees in His grace.

Sarvalokacharin

ॐ श्री सर्वलोकचारिणे नमः

Wanderer

Lord Hanuman, gifted with the speed of the wind, can fly at will to any place, with the ability to grow or reduce in size as and when the situation demands. He is seen everywhere as He loves to wander everywhere.

Manojava

ॐ श्री मनोजवाय नमः
Speed Like Wind

Attributed with the speed of wind, inherited from His father, Wind-God, Lord Hanuman leaped across the sea to reach Lanka, and moved like the wind in search of Sita, finally locating her in the Ashoka grove.

Parijata Tarumoolastha

ॐ श्री पारिजात तरूमूलस्थाय नमः

*Resides Under
The Parijata Tree*

To curtail the arrogance of the Sudarshan Chakra and Satyabhama, Lord Hanuman was summoned under the Parijata tree. His mission was successfully accomplished thus sanctifying the ground under the tree.

Sarvamantra Swaroopavat

ॐ श्री सर्वमंत्र स्वरूपवते नमः

Possessor Of All Hymns

Lord Hanuman is a Master of all branches of knowledge. He is very fond of hymns, being a good singer Himself. His favourite hymns are those on His beloved Master, Lord Rama, whose very name brings bliss to Him.

Sarvatantra Swaroopin

ॐ श्री सर्वतंत्र स्वरूपिणे नमः

Shape Of All Hymns

The auspiciously radiant Lord Hanuman is well-versed in hymns and is ever chanting them in praise of His beloved Lord Rama. Since He has the ability to take any form at will, He also manifests as hymns.

Sarvayantratmaka

ॐ श्री सर्वयंत्रात्मकाय नमः

Dweller In All Yantras

The erudite and intelligent Lord Hanuman is well-versed in all *tantras*, *mantras* and *yantras*, and resides in all yantras.

Kapeeshwara

ॐ श्री कपीश्वराय नमः

Lord Of The Monkeys

As the exalted Lord of the monkeys, Lord Hanuman is the lifelong slave of Lord Rama. He serves Him with devotion and with His army of monkeys, vanquishes the demons of Lanka.

Mahakaya

ॐ श्री महाकायाय नमः

Gigantic

The strong-limbed, golden-hued Lord Hanuman has a magnificent physique. Strong and sturdy, He is soft-spoken and calm towards His devotees, and to the demons He is a cause of terror and dread.

Sarvarogahara

ॐ श्री सर्वरोगहराय नमः
Reliever Of All Ailments

Lord Hanuman destroys all sorrows and afflictions. A mere chant of His name ends all agonies and ill-health. By devoting one's attention faithfully to His visage, one is instantly cured of any health problem.

Prabhav

ॐ श्री प्रभावे नमः

Popular Lord

Lord Hanuman's sincere devotion to Lord Rama makes Him divinely lovable and worthy of worship. He dispels distress, and is considered to be very popular and auspicious.

Batna Siddhikara

ॐ श्री बत्न सिद्धिकराय नमः

Granter Of Strength

Also called Sundar due to His beautiful, strong and sturdy physique, Lord Hanuman is endowed with extraordinary strength inherited from His father, Wind-God, and as such, He grants strength to His devotees.

Sarvavidyasampat Pradayaka

ॐ श्री सर्वविद्यासंपत् प्रदायकाय नमः

Granter Of Knowledge And Wisdom

Lord Hanuman is well-learned, very intelligent and extremely devoted, and grants this treasured virtue to His faithful devotees.

Kapisenanayaka

ॐ श्री कपिसेननायकाय नमः

Chief Of The Monkey Army

As the General and Commander of the army of Sugreeva's monkey clan, Lord Hanuman sets out with His army in search of Sita. Later, He commands this army in the battle against Ravana and the other demons.

Bhavishya Chaturanana

ॐ श्री भविष्यच्चतुराननाय नमः

Aware Of Future Happenings

Lord Hanuman's wisdom and knowledge are unfathomable. All the three worlds are fulfilled with His glory, and He is aware of all future happenings.

Kumarabrahmacharin

ॐ श्री कुमारब्रह्मचारिणे नमः
Youthful Bachelor

Lord Hanuman the eternal youthful bachelor, is an adorable God. Devotees salute this bachelorhood and He blesses them to fulfil all their wishes.

Ratnakundala Deeptimat

ॐ श्री रत्नकुण्डल दीप्तिमते नमः

Wearing Gem-Studded Earrings

The dynamic and golden-hued darling Son of Pawana, Wind-God, Lord Hanuman has bright eyes and wears gem-studded earrings that enhance His enchanting personality.

Chanchaladwala Sanabdwalambamana Shikhojwala

ॐ श्री चंचलद्वाल सनद्धलंबमान शिखोज्वलाय नमः

Long-Tailed, Glittering Tail Suspended Above The Head

Lord Hanuman is courageous and valiant. With a long, glittering tail, that is mostly suspended above His head, He charms everyone.

Gandharvavidya Tatvagnana

ॐ श्री गंधर्वविद्या तत्वज्ञान नमः

Exponent In The Art Of Celestials

Lord Hanuman has complete control of His mind and senses. Being an exponent in the arts and in all branches of knowledge, He is the bestower of the noblest form of devotion.

Mahabala Parakrama

ॐ श्री महाबल पराक्रमाय नमः

Of Great Strength

The sturdy, robust, strong Son of Wind-God, Lord Hanuman is the repository of immense power and strength, with a sinuous body dazzling like gold.

Karagrihavimoktri

ॐ श्री कारागृहविमोक्त्रे नमः

One Who Frees From Imprisonment

Lord Hanuman is instrumental in freeing Lord Rama and Lakshmana from the noose of a serpent; from Ahiravana who had abducted them; and also Sita from Ravana.

Shrinkhalabandha Mochaka

ॐ श्री शृंखलाबंध मोचकाय नमः

Reliever From A Chain Of Distresses

Lord Hanuman, who is reputed to protect His most faithful devotees, relieves them from the chain of distresses. Hence, is also known as the distress-dispelling Lord.

Sagarotharaka

ॐ श्री सागरोत्तारकाय नमः

Leapt Across The Ocean

On Sugreeva's advice a squad of monkeys went in search of Sita, reaching the seashore without any trace of her. Undaunted by the vast stretch of water, Lord Hanuman took a mighty leap across the ocean to reach Lanka in a trice, where He ultimately found Sita.

Pragnya

ॐ श्री प्रज्ञाय नमः
Scholar

As an exalted scholar, Lord Hanuman is well-versed in all branches of knowledge. His intelligence and chaste conduct are salient traits of His greatness, for He is verily a limitless fountain of divine knowledge.

Ramadhuta

ॐ श्री रामदूताय नमः
Ambassador Of Rama

Lord Hanuman is the renowned messenger of Lord Rama, and well-versed in the duties of an ambassador, eruditely discoursing on the code of conduct of a messenger. He is always ready to accomplish any job commanded by His Lord.

Pratapavat

ॐ श्री प्रतापवते नमः

Known For Valour

The strong-armed, golden-hued Lord Hanuman is reputed for His valour and daring. He is fearless when He confronts Ravana in his court, and bravely fights the demons, finally slaying them.

Vanara

ॐ श्री वानराय नमः

Monkey

Lord Hanuman is a magnanimous monkey God. He is immortal and revered by all. He is most chaste, valiant and learned among the warriors, and is said to possess divine knowledge.

Kesarisuta

ॐ श्री केसरीसुताय नमः
Son Of Kesari

Lord Hanuman is the immensely powerful Son of Kesari, the monkey chieftain, and of Anjani, the daughter of the monkey lord, Kunjar. He is very courageous and is the Lord of the monkey warriors.

Sitashoka Nivarana

ॐ श्री सीताशोक निवारणाय नमः

Destroyer Of Sita's Sorrow

On finding Sita in Ashoka grove, he gave her Lord Rama's ring along with glad tidings, assuring her that Lord Rama is on His way to rescue her. Thus, He brings her relief from distress and despair.

Anjanagarbhasambhoota

ॐ श्री अंजनागर्भसंभूताय नमः

Born Of Anjani

The most virtuous and noble of the monkey warriors, Lord Hanuman is born of Anjani who was blessed to carry Him in her womb. As her darling Son, He serves her as faithfully as He serves Lord Rama.

Balarka Sadrishanana

ॐ श्री बालार्क सदृशाननाय नमः

Like The Rising Sun

Lord Hanuman, the Lord of the monkey clan, is like the rising sun, dazzling like a mountain of gold. He sets Lanka ablaze with His burning tail, creating havoc among the demons.

Vibheeshanapriyakara

ॐ श्री विभीषणप्रियकराय नमः

Beloved Of Vibheeshana

Lord Hanuman befriends Vibheeshana, the brother of Ravana. Vibheeshana is noble, and realising the sinful deeds of Ravana, reveals to Lord Hanuman the whereabouts of Sita, thus becoming an ally of Lord Rama.

Dashagreeva Kulantaka

ॐ श्री दशग्रीवकुलान्तकाय नमः

Slayer Of The Ten-Headed Ravana's Race

The destroyer of wickedness and of all that is evil, is Lord Hanuman, who brow beats the ten-headed Ravana and his race, thus paving the way for the delightful reunion of Lord Rama and Sita.

Lakshmana Pranadatre

ॐ श्री लक्ष्मणप्राणदात्रे नमः

Reviver Of Lakshmana's Life

When Lakshmana was fatally wounded, on the advice of the physician, Lord Hanuman went to the Himalayas to fetch the sanjeevani herb. Not being able to recognise the herb, He lifted the whole hill and brought it in time to revive Lakshmana.

Vajrakaya

ॐ श्री वज्रकायाय नमः
Sturdy Like Metal

Lord Hanuman, the beloved Sun of Anjani and Kesari, is as strong and sturdy as a thunderbolt, immune to any blow. He is gigantic and His arms are powerfully strong.

Mahadhyutay

ॐ श्री महाद्युतये नमः
Most Radiant

The auspicious-visaged Lord of the monkey clan, Lord Hanuman is supremely intelligent and is an ocean of patience. He wears a crown that symbolises His scholarly skills and divine intelligence, exuding radiance like the bright rays of the sun.

Chiranjeevin

ॐ श्री चिरंजीविने नमः
Eternal Being

After swallowing the sun as a boy, and then releasing it on being entreated by the gods, He was blessed by Indra with immortality, that as long as Lord Rama's name survives on earth, He too shall remain alive on earth.

Rama Bhakta

ॐ श्री राम भक्ताय नमः
Devoted To Rama

While Lord Rama is the monkey God's chosen deity, the latter is Lord Rama's most ardent devotee. He rejoices in the happiness of His Lord and suffers the agony that His Lord has to bear.

Daityakarya Vidhyataka

ॐ श्री दैत्यकार्य विद्यातकाय नमः

Destroyer Of All Demonic Activities

Being the destroyer of all evil spirits, He dispels all distresses. Lord Hanuman is the nemesis for the demons and everything that stands for evil.

Akshahantri

ॐ श्री अक्षहंत्रे नमः

Slayer Of Aksha

As the Lord of all monkeys, Lord Hanuman vanquished the son of Ravana, Aksha, fighting single-handedly in the Ashoka grove.

Kalanabha

ॐ श्री कालानाभाय नमः
Controller Of Time

With immense power and strength, Lord Hanuman is the controller of time. Every movement in the universe is at His will, and His movements are like the wind, fast and powerful, for He is the illustrious Son of Wind-God.

Kanchanabha

ॐ श्री कांचनाभाय नमः

Golden-Hued Body

Lord Hanuman has a dazzling red form, like the rising sun at dawn. His body shines like a mountain of gold, whose golden-hued tail set fire to Ravana's empire in Lanka.

Panchavaktra

ॐ श्री पंचवक्त्राय नमः
Five-Faced

Lord Hanuman, the auspicious-visaged deity, is an embodiment of all that ensures the welfare of humanity. Taking any form at will, He is five-faced at times—all-knowing, all-seeing and fully aware of everything.

Mahatapas

ॐ श्री महातपसे नमः

Great Meditator

The most devoted and distress-dispelling slave of Lord Rama is Lord Hanuman. He meditates deeply, His focus on the lotus feet of His beloved master, Lord Rama.

Lankineebhanjana

ॐ श्री लंकिणीभंजनाय नमः

Slayer Of Lankini

When Lord Hanuman was on His way to Lanka in search of Sita, He was waylaid by the demoness Lankini. He kicked her so hard that she died instantly, being relieved of her curse and attaining salvation.

Shrimat

ॐ श्री श्रीमते नमः

Revered

Lord Hanuman, the most brilliant and intelligent monkey warrior, is most revered and He is devoted to Lord Rama, owing His very existence to Him. He is most adorable and popular amongst His devotees.

Simhikaprana Bhanjana

ॐ श्री सिंहिकाप्राण भंजनाय नमः

Slayer Of Simhika

The mighty Lord Hanuman leaped across the ocean in search of Sita. Simhika, an ogress, and mother of Rahu, opened her mouth wide to swallow the Lord, but He contracted, entered her mouth, ripped her apart and thus slew her.

Gandhamadhanashailastha

ॐ श्री गंधमाधनशैलस्थाय नमः

Dweller of Gandhamadhana

When Lord Rama halted at Gandhamadhana Mount to atone for slaying Ravana, a Brahmin, Lord Hanuman installed a *Shivalinga* there to worship. Since then, the place has been sanctified by Lord Hanuman's presence.

Lankapuravidahaka

ॐ श्री लंकापुरविदाहकाय नमः

He Who Burnt Lanka

Lord Hanuman, with His tail burning in all its glory, set fire to the whole of Lanka, to the delight of the gods, fluttering that burning flag-like tail high in the sky as a sign of victory.

Sugreeva Sachiva

ॐ श्री सुग्रीव सचिवाय नमः

Minister Of Sugreeva

As the minister of Sugreeva, Lord Hanuman commands the army of monkey warriors in the battle against Ravana's demons. He is instrumental in establishing a strong bond between Lord Rama and Sugreeva.

Dheera

ॐ श्री धीराय नमः
Valiant

As the great and mighty Son of Wind-God, Lord Hanuman is known for His valour, intelligence and determination, and, above all, for His devotion to Lord Rama. As the valiant monkey warrior, He is the scourge of His enemies.

Shoora

ॐ श्री शूराये नमः
Bold

Known for His boldness and immense strength, Lord Hanuman is propitiated by His devotees, seeking His blessings and grace, to make them fearless and righteous in their actions.

Daithyakulantaka

ॐ श्री दैत्यकुलान्तकाय नमः

Destroyer Of Demons

Lord Hanuman, strong and gigantic, is the veritable cause for the death of demons like Prince Akshaya, the demoness Lankini, and others.

Surarchita

ॐ श्री सुरार्चिताय नमः

Worshipped By Celestials

Lord Hanuman is worshipped by celestials, the great seers and sages, Brahma and the other gods, and also great poets who describe His glory in glowing terms. It is difficult to fathom His glory.

Mahatejas

ॐ श्री महातेजसे नमः

Most Radiant

Lord Hanuman is resplendent in all His glory with a radiant and divine form that changes at will. The radiance of His divine personality is immensely beautiful.

Ramachoodamaniprada

ॐ श्री रामचूड़ामणिप्रदाय नमः

Deliverer Of Rama's Ring

The darling devotee of Lord Rama, in whose heart He dwells is Lord Hanuman. Lord Rama, entrusts Him with His ring, asking Him to deliver it to His wife, Sita, as a mark of His identification.

Kamaroopin

ॐ श्री कामरूपिणे नमः

Changing Form At Will

Known for His illimitable physical power, Lord Hanuman changes His form and size as the situation demands, and thus protects His beloved faithfuls.

Pingalaksha

ॐ श्री पिंगळाक्षाय नमः
Pink-Eyed

Lord Hanuman, with a gigantic physique and strong arms, is gentleness personified. His pink eyes exude tenderness and compassion for the devotees.

Vardhimainakapoojita

ॐ श्री वार्धिमैनाकपूजिताय नमः

Worshipped By Mynaka Hill

Born as the darling Son of Wind-God, Lord Hanuman is gifted with the power and speed of His father. When Lord Hanuman was crossing the ocean in search of Sita, Mynaka Hill rose up to facilitate the Lord to rest awhile.

Kabalikrita Martanda Mandala

ॐ श्री कबलीकृत मार्तांड मंडलाय नमः

Swallower Of The Sun

Most valiant and strong, Lord Hanuman, unaware of His strength, flew up to the sun and swallowed it, till, at the bequest of the gods, He released it.

Vijitendriya

ॐ श्री विजितेंद्रियाय नमः

Controller Of The Senses

Lord Hanuman is the master of all the senses and can control them. Being a limitless mine of virtues, He controls the destiny of all, and is aware of all that is to happen.

Ramasugreeva Sandhatri

ॐ श्री रामसुग्रीव सन्धात्रे नमः

Mediator Between Rama and Sugreeva

Lord Hanuman, the most faithful and trustworthy follower of Lord Rama, is instrumental in establishing a strong friendship between His Lord and Sugreeva, the chief of the monkey clan.

Maharavanamardhana

ॐ श्री महारावणमर्दनाय नमः

Slayer Of The Famous Ravana

Lord Hanuman spelled doom for the arrogant Ravana when the latter had the monkey Lord's tail set on fire, for since then, Lord Hanuman was the veritable cause of downfall and his death.

Sphatikabha

ॐ श्री स्फटिकाभाय नमः

Crystal-Clear

Lord Hanuman is a mine of virtue, and His love and devotion for Lord Rama is pure and crystal-clear like the best of gems, radiating love and glory, and evoking inspiration and reverence in all.

Vagadheeksha

ॐ श्री वागधीक्षाय नमः

Lord Of Spokespeople

Lord Hanuman is well-versed in all branches of knowledge. When He swallowed the sun as a young boy, He was entreated by the gods to release it. As a boon the Sun-God blessed Him with intelligence and divine knowledge, making Him the Lord of spokespeople.

Navavyakriti Pandita

ॐ श्री नवव्याकृति पंडिताय नमः

Skilful Scholar

Lord Hanuman is blessed with great intelligence and skills that help Him to serve Lord Rama. He is well-versed in Sanskrit, being thorough with the nine arts that makes one a scholar, and is a master in all branches of knowledge.

Chaturbahav

ॐ श्री चतुर्बाहवे नमः
Four-Armed

Lord Hanuman, who is blessed with the ability to change His form as He wills, uses His mighty arms for slaying enemies, and with the thunderbolt-like mace creates a feeling of dread in them.

Deenabandhav

ॐ श्री दीनबन्धवे नमः

Protector Of The Downtrodden

With Lord Hanuman as the Protector and Friend of the downtrodden, one need fear nothing in the world. All the happiness and felicity of the world are achievable only when one seeks refuge in His grace.

Mahatman

ॐ श्री महात्मने नमः

Supreme Being

Believed to be the eleventh incarnation of Rudra (Shiva), Lord Hanuman is the Supreme Being and Lord Rama expresses His infinite gratitude to Him. He is worshipped by millions all over the world.

Bhaktavatsala

ॐ श्री भक्तवत्सलाय नमः
Protector Of Devotees

Lord Hanuman protects all His devotees from the most deadly demons and all that is evil. He answers everyone's prayers for protection and saves them from evil. Therefore, He is also known as Sankat Mochan.

Sanjeevana Nagahatri

ॐ श्री संजीवननगहत्रे नमः

Bearer Of Sanjeevani Mount

Lakshmana, fatally wounded by Meghanad, Ravana's son, lies unconscious on the battlefield. On the physician's advice Lord Hanuman goes to the Himalayas to fetch the sanjeevani herb. Not recognising the herb, He carries the Sanjeevani mount to the battlefield in time to save his life.

Shuchay

ॐ श्री शुचये नमः

Chaste

Well-versed in Sanskrit and as a great scholar, Lord Hanuman has a profound knowledge of future happenings. He is chaste in His speech, action and behaviour, endearing Himself to His beloved Master, Lord Rama.

Vagmin

ॐ श्री वाग्मिने नमः

Spokesman

Lord Hanuman is the sentinel to the access of Lord Rama. Without His support no aspirant can ever hope to have the grace of Lord Rama. As His spokesman, Lord Hanuman fulfils His job admirably and faithfully.

Dhruddavrata

ॐ श्री दृढ़व्रताय नमः
Strong-Willed Mediator

Lord Hanuman, who forever serves His Lord Rama, meditates very deeply with a strong will and concentration, His focus being on His Lord.

Kalanemi Pramathana

ॐ श्री कालनेमि प्रमथनाय नमः

Slayer of Kalanemi

When Lord Hanuman went to fetch the sanjeevani herb to revive Lakshmana, the demon Kalanemi intended to kill Him, but in the process was killed by the Lord.

Harimarkatamarkata

ॐ श्री हरिमर्कटमर्कटाय नमः

Lord Of Monkeys

Son of Kesari, the monkey chieftain, the valiant and sturdy Hanuman is the Lord of the monkey warriors, leading them in a battle against the clan of Ravana. His glory gets enhanced by the gratefulness of His beloved Rama.

Danta

ॐ श्री दाँताय नमः

Calm

As the humble slave of Lord Rama, Lord Hanuman dedicates all His services to His Lord with love and humility. Though highly intelligent and erudite, He is never arrogant, and His calm and composed appearance causes one to repose one's total faith in Him.

Shanta

ॐ श्री शांताय नमः
Very Composed

Always very active and vivacious, Lord Hanuman is peace and calm personified. He moves like the wind and prances around, but all done with sedateness and composure that make Him so dignified.

Prasannatman

ॐ श्री प्रसन्नात्मने नमः
Cheerful

The humble and calm Lord Hanuman is ever cheerful, even in the face of adversity. When His favourite lord is lying unconscious, He cheerfully sets about bringing Him back to consciousness. He is forever cheerful chanting Lord Rama's name.

Shatakanttamadapahat

ॐ श्री शतकंठमदापहते नमः

Destroyer Of Shatakantta's Arrogance

Lord Hanuman, renowned for His skill in changing His form at will, was instrumental in destroying the arrogance of Shatakantta.

Yogin

ॐ श्री योगिने नमः

Saint

Lord Hanuman blesses the truly noble devotees. He is saintly in His appearance, with saffron paste anointed all over His body. His being radiates divine light and glows in eternal splendour.

Ramakathalola

ॐ श्री रामकथालोलाय नमः

*Loves Listening
To Rama's Story*

The auspicious-visaged Lord Hanuman, whose chosen deity is Lord Rama, never tires of listening to the stories of His Master. When His Lord is praised, He feels thrilled and elated, and chants His name cheerfully.

Sitanveshana Pandita

ॐ श्री सीतान्वेषण पण्डिताय नमः

Skilful in Finding Sita's Whereabouts

When all the monkeys fail to locate the whereabouts of Sita, Lord Hanuman leaps across the ocean to Lanka, and using His intelligence and skills traces her to the Ashoka grove.

Vajranakha

ॐ श्री वज्रनखाय नमः

Strong-Nailed

When Lord Hanuman reaches the Ashoka grove and sees the demonesses harassing Sita, He uproots the dense and beautiful trees with His strong hands, using His strong nails to scratch and maul the demons who come in His way.

Rudraveerya Samudbhava

ॐ श्री रूद्रवीर्य समुद्भवाय नमः
Born Of Shiva

When the Ocean of milk was churned and Lord Vishnu took the form of Mohini, Lord Shiva got very attracted to her. Not wanting His seed to go waste, Anjani accepted it and bore Lord Shiva's son, Hanuman.

Indrajit Prahitamogha Brahmastra Vinivaraka

ॐ श्री इंद्रजित प्रहितमोघ ब्रह्मास्त्र विनिवारकाय नमः

Destroyer Of The Effect Of Indrajit's Brahmastra

When Lord Hanuman created havoc in the Ashoka grove, Indrajit hurled his Bramhastra, the divine missile created by Brahma, to vanquish him. But Hanuman absorbed the shock of this deadly weapon.

Parthadhwajagra Samvasin

ॐ श्री पार्थध्वजाग्र संवासिने नमः

Having Foremost Place On Arjuna's Flag

When Lord Hanuman punctured Arjuna's bloated ego, Arjuna entreated Him to forgive him and help him in fighting the Kauravas. He promised and invisibly took position on Arjuna's flag.

Sharapanjarabhedaka

ॐ श्री शरपंजरभेदकाय नमः

Destroyer Of The Nest Made Of Arrows

When Ravana's men attacked Lord Hanuman with arrows He counter-attacked them with His weapons. So they built a nest of arrows around them as a safeguard, Which He destroyed.

Dashabahav

ॐ श्री दशबाहवे नमः

Ten-Armed

He is the veritable death for the demon prince, Akshaya, and with His mighty arms, destroys all that spells evil. Gifted with the power and strength of Vayu, His father, the Wind-God, He evokes fear in His enemies.

Lokapoojya

ॐ श्री लोकपूज्याय नमः
Worshipped By The Universe

Lord Hanuman is the darling of the Supreme Lord Rama. He is devoutly worshipped by the entire universe, being virtuous and Himself devoted in His services to Lord Rama. Through Him one can attain Lord Rama.

Jambavatpreeti Vardhana

ॐ श्री जांबवत्प्रीति वर्धनाय नमः

Winning Jambavana's Love

Lord Hanuman, a mine of virtues and knowledge, won the love and respect of Jambavan, the chief of the bears, by His humble and subservient demeanour.

Sitasameta Ramapadaseva Dhurandhara

ॐ श्री सीतासमेत श्रीरामपादसेवाधुरंधराय नमः

Always Engrossed In Rama's Service

Noted for His dedicated services to His beloved Lord Rama and likewise to Sita, Lord Hanuman totally surrenders on to Him, merging His identity with His chosen Lord.